A Baker's Dozen

Glimpses of Hope and Rays of Light For the Road

NICK RINGMA

Copyright © 2014 by Nick Ringma. 541430
Library of Congress Control Number: 2014904051

ISBN: Softcover   978-1-4931-7914-5
        Hardcover   978-1-4931-7913-8
        EBook   978-1-4931-7915-2

This is a work of fiction. Names, characters,
places and incidents either are the product of the
author's imagination or are used fictitiously, and any
resemblance to any actual persons, living or dead,
events, or locales is entirely coincidental.

Rev. date: 03/15/2014

To order additional copies of this book, contact:
Xlibris LLC
1-888-795-4274
www.Xlibris.com
Orders@Xlibris.com

Acknowledgements

These rays of light on the journey have their roots in many conversations along the way. However, the enfolding arms of four communities made the journey an adventure: the community of recovery at the Last Door (www.lastdoor.org), the community of faith at Willoughby Church (www.willoughbychurch.com), the community of support and service in Narcotics Anonymous (www.na.org), and most lovingly, the community of family and friends that carried me.

There are many ears and hearts that have shared this journey—and to each of you, a special thank-you. My friends, my family, and my colleagues have all contributed to this work knowingly or unknowingly. The on-the-road contributions and conversations with David and Louise have focused ideas and actions. Margaret, who lived through the past, survives the daily present and carries me with hope into an unknown future, which has been both impetus and inspiration. Age has a way of tumbling remembrance at your feet, and the loss of my friends is carried in sentences, allusions, and references.

The staff team at the Last Door Recovery Society was having a conversation about changes in addictions treatment—how recovery and healing comes from living life in community as restored persons. A spiritual awakening through laughter, hope, and restoration rebuilds lives according to the plan, a redemptive understanding of God!

Your family member, friend, or partner deserves a better outcome than a statistical death. This book is for each one still suffering—that they too might know that recovery works to create lives of abstinence filled with gratitude.

Prologue

This book is a collection of images, poems, and stories that stretch beyond the boundaries of traditional spiritual practice. This is the art of living—synchronized with the nurturing of heart and mind for devotion and stretching to reach an awakening of love, joy, pain, laughter, sorrow, and integrity. Each entry is focused by the eyes of recovery. Freedom from self was brought to action by the twelve steps and liberated in community by coffee, conversation, and care at the Doorstep of Last Door and echoed in the Doorways of the world. I have spent years writing advertising scripts, liturgies, poems, documents, business plans, and nonsense. This collection was fun. Each entry in this journal has its roots in some coffee bar, airport, beach, meeting, church, or wandering conversation. Each was a gift along the way.

In early recovery from addiction, I had the opportunity to live in and around the Last Door Recovery Community. I was drafted for service to the community of recovering persons, and after years of clinical practice, I took the opportunity to create this collection of snippets to mark the thirty years of a recovery community consistently and progressively moving beyond "step work" to living and enjoying life. Last Door is more than a treatment centre. Last Door is a community of recovering persons that has held to abstinence principles, steadfastly believing that if a person seeking recovery was willing to do whatever it takes, they could get well. These stories are a tribute to all who pioneered recovery from drugs, alcohol, and self—an acknowledgement of those who are living by spiritual principles as they reach toward virtue on the journey.

There is an old English idiom called a baker's dozen. The Scuttlebutt and Wikipedia call it a regular dozen, plus one extra item thrown in for good measure. I grew up in a bakery and only once witnessed such generosity. Earning a living baking was hard work, and every penny was precious. My father was a pastry chef and proudly maintained that if people wanted something special, they would be willing to pay for it. Over the years, his axiom has proven correct. On the tenth anniversary of Glendale Bakery, he elected to share his gratitude with his customers. He had a "baker's dozen" sale. Simply buy twelve and get the thirteenth one free. Now as sales went, it was no cash-register-ringing success; but as gestures go, it was generous. In twelve-step communities, there are no teachers, no masters, no leaders. Recovery is a process of communal wisdom garnered by intentionally working each of the twelve steps to effect personal change. With time and effort, growing self-awareness changes beliefs, behaviours, and attitudes. Like the baker's dozen, this is one occasion where I will step beyond the simple dozen-step world and deliver a thirteenth snippet for Last Door measure! A community where "going the extra mile" was more than a slogan, where step-work was a doorway to a journey of recovery.

EXPERIENCE

1 *Stepping Out*

OK, the evening was like most others. We walked home from church laughing about how we'd frustrated the dominie, laughing about how we'd poked the skin of a holy man—all more than funny in my adolescent mind. It was the stage from which I would launch a thousand rebellious variations: the fireworks in the mailbox, the gas across the road, the midnight border crossing, the drunken vessel charters, the speeding traps and radar detectors, the flag persons and the seat belts, and the repeated using in treatment. The catechism teacher of my youth probably knew something about obedience and rebelliousness that I was not ready to learn. In the lessons I learned, there was a clear and steadfast "world and life" view that valued creation and all its creatures.

Time in and out of treatment merged with that burr of constant rebellion. No one was going to tell me what to do! Interventions, shotgun clauses, payment pauses, family pledges, psychotic flashes, rolled-up carpets, and clipped credit cards all came and went like ever-passing flashes of interference. No one could stop me. I was prayed for and over, and the memorized catechism lessons were fading to black. Perched in a rented downtown room between the chocolate-drink bottles and the darker-than-curtains shady characters, I sat behind a keyboard (stolen from what used to be my house), and I started to type. The words were not flowing, letters not making sense. Even the characters left—melancholy was not their trip.

Over several hours with a reinforced drug supply, I typed my own funeral service. Somewhere in there between the opening hymn and the doxology, I placed a catechism lesson. The holy man had asked from the book, "What is true faith?" I answered from memory, "It is a sure knowledge and firm confidence . . ." A moment of hope before the dope was gone. I was not alone.

A knock on the door. The kids had come to drag their father away from terminal action and a word pyre, away from the despair of self-pity. Their presence that "sure knowledge." God cares. Then with a revived firm confidence, I had hope again—hope that this time it might work. Weeks later in a detox centre, the words of the catechism lesson—"What is your only comfort in life and death?"—started to pinch. For years, I thought I was my only comfort, or she was my only comfort. Or fermented grapes were my only comfort, or some other fluid was my Southern Comfort. Or some poked, toked, or smoked powder was my comfort or money or prestige or, more subtly, the addiction to power or food. I flew all over the world looking for comfort, never satiated. The lessons were in the catechism! The lessons were probably in the package of lessons in kindergarten: be nice, share, love, be kind, look after, clean up your own mess, nap time. Sitting alone trying to detox, I was assessing when life had become unmanageable. When had I lost control?

The answer was somewhere between kindergarten and catechism. The answer was in my inability to follow the lesson plan. I rewrote the lesson plan only to run headlong into the tablets confirming that certain things are engraved in stone, carved by the hands of friends and carried in the arms of family. The holy man knew about surrender. I had to learn that breaking tablets of stone didn't change the words.

2 *Stepping To*

It was some months before I was part of a recovery fellowship and the idea of a higher power started to pinch. The first pinch was on my own cheeks: here I am again, my life in a puddle of selfish tears, my family pushing me out of the door again, and no one left to use with. I was alone. I had money, and I had dope—but I was the kind of *alone* that money couldn't fix. No one wanted to watch me die, watch me kill myself. On the inside, I was as good as dead. I didn't care. Someone suggested I go to a meeting and listen. OK, there was enough desperation that I went to an NA meeting.

I remember sitting in the meeting with a fellow junkie. Laundry was in the Laundromat around the corner. Dope was coming soon. Juice and chocolate milk stained our costumes, the remnants of chaos covering us—and then someone started talking about having learned to live without drugs, and someone else said that they had found freedom. We were obviously in the wrong room. These guys were talking about change. There wasn't a ray of hope that this might work—OK, a glimmer. I stole a Basic Text from the literature table and tucked it under my jacket. The temperature was twenty-six degrees centigrade outside, and I was wearing a jacket. This coming-to-believe stuff sometimes starts with a fragment—a twisted turn of fate. Over the years, I've heard people say, "This won't work for me" or "That's not how I see it" or "That's just bullshit." My favourite is the "But my situation is not like anyone else's." The very argument, the struggle to discount any program of recovery, is the beginning of the journey that leads to belief that this stuff might work. My experience is that faith requires a good dose of doubt, a solid case of cynicism, and appropriate portions of pain and love.

I remember one Saturday morning, fifty years ago, when the power failed. I was working in the bakery with trays of perishable goods, some requiring refrigeration and others waiting for baking. When the power fails—ready or not—stuff will rot.

Baking, like recovery, needs regular inputs of discipline, the ferment of wisdom, and power to yield quality goods. Baking is one extended chemical transformation. Nobody wants stale goods. But this was fifty years ago. The most frustrating side effect of a power failure in our time might be the loss of Internet connectivity. When power fails, a lot of conversations, messages, tweets, and Flickrs are left dangling. Yet I keep typing, knowing the power will come back on soon—the hope that "knows" about some possibility of light again. I remember when the lights came on in the bakery, every action was focused on preserving the pastries. I now know that in recovery, when the lights go on, when power shows up, it takes action to move through doubt to faith.

Ten years ago on a sweat-banging Delhi street, four fair friends and a sheikh driver launched a four-day road trip to see the sights. The bright Diwali-orange turban was not a clue. Ten minutes into the awkward silence of four passengers in a minivan, the traffic cleared, and we rolled forward, settling back for what was to be a crawling getting-there. Curiosity fingered through the knobs and buttons and papers in the van, looking for something in the moment to play with—a distraction. The pamphlet was carefully placed between the seats with the other important papers—the NA fellowship logo. Not just any brochure, this was a glistening convention schedule. I looked at Raghbir, and he looked at us. We laughed at how God was a gag writer!

Halfway around the globe and the one of one billion persons who was our driver had a home group and a service position in the fellowship of Narcotics Anonymous. There is a spiritual connection between us that is summarized in the week ending, the meeting-closing Serenity Prayer chanted as we circled the banyan tree. The power in the bakery and the power of the closing prayer reminded me that God is closer than I ever imagined.

3 Stepping Free

The ice storm was severe. Driving was impossible. Between the coating-everything drizzle and the snapping trees, survival was at risk. The rental car was sliding down the incline like an out-of-control skier, wheels locked and chattering across the ice-polished pavement. Stopping would come with a crash in the slow-motion world of accidents. Letting go of the brakes, surrendering control, the car reoriented and naturally lined up with the fall line of the hill, tires scratching for pavement and against hope, slowing as the bottom of the hill came closer—stopping just in time. Lifesaving moments are amazing. That was twenty years ago.

Ten years ago, I saw a scratched blue bodyboard for rent. In between the curls of the surf and the waves of wind, he hustled his board for a few dollars per hour. The idea was not new, nor was the gesture magnanimous. The ten-year-old sun-warmed-and-worn merchant had all the moves: $3 an hour, $5 for two hours, and $10 for a whole day. He saw my white skin going pink the first hours there and made the proposition. I could have his board for the whole week for $40. Now I wasn't a novice to the way of boards and words and negotiations, but this kid was quick.

Those white-master-guilt thoughts emerged just as the price started to drop and then the phone rang—an interruption of divine magnitude. The voice said words about dying and finding his body on the side of the road and how they saw his bike tracks. Dead. I lost interest in the boards and submerged into the grief of the moment. My brother-in-law was dead. The announcement was an intrusive quake in the sun-soaked serenity. I was struck by a spiritual reality. I was alive. Bill had joined the community of recovering persons a year after I had. He died clean because someone rescued me.

In the local board shop, bodyboards were selling for $30 and cheap ones for $19. I bought one of each and went back to the boy on the beach later that afternoon. The sun was hot and the beach crowded. I gave him the two boards and had him try renting them out. The three boards were all out at one time! He grossed some $40 that afternoon, said he'd never made that much money. He offered me $30 for my two boards and was about to head home when I tapped him on the shoulder and told him to come with me. We walked over to the board shop, and I asked him which the best board was. He pointed to a white one with a silver logo. It was $50. I asked him if people would pay more for that board. He shrugged. "Not tourists, but real boarders would."

With the extra board topping the stack on his wagon, he headed home ready for the next morning. That evening, I found a bright yellow umbrella and had the local artist letter it overnight: *Bobbie's Body Boards*. By noon, all the boards were out on four-hour rentals. Bobbie had four boards, a sign, and a beach. He was smiling.

Oh, and all that news about brother Bill wasn't that big anymore, and the memories of the night in the ice storm melted with the memory of the car piloted to safety by someone—some power that thought I needed a break. Never made the spiritual connection till I saw the kid smile at me. Believing happens long before insight, before understanding.

4 *Stepping Forth*

I could never be wrong. A whole life lived being right. The discussion stopping "I know." In the introspection of a fourth step, there is opportunity for a balanced self-awareness, an inventory of all that drives and drags in my life. Trying to find a single apt metaphor for the insight of recovery created panic.

I had spent years in retail counting inventory and detailing the values as well as marking down the unsalable and broken items, but applying those audit-reliable guidelines to the stack of chaos called character was a daunting task. Years in retail taught me a valuable lesson about the accuracy of an inventory. Whenever we hired a "professional" agency to take inventory, they would routinely miss the defective items or the incomplete packages. They really were not aware of all the items required to make a Walkman work. A Walkman without an earpiece produces as much sound as a roll of cotton. In the muffled silence is the metaphor.

To take inventory, my own inventory, I need to see exactly where the disconnects are, where the missing pieces go, and how the packaging keeps getting ripped open. Years in retail had produced a mantra, "Stock taking stinks." T-shirts were screened with STS slogans and contests abounded for accuracy and timeliness. When the tally sheets were replaced with computer printouts and, later, with handheld scanners, change was promoted as improving accuracy and getting results quicker. My memory has it that a pen and a piece of paper were as fast and accurate as any device, form, grid, or estimate. There were no shortcuts.

One year, we sold a division of a company, and the inventory had to be valued at midnight, October 31. Vancouver is not inclined to many severe storms, but this was the night of exception. A gale-force special rolled across Burrard Inlet and powered down the city. Candles and flashlights and 40 percent of the staff team, and the job got done. Stock taking stinks but is essential for establishing value and understanding the nature of the asset. This taking-personal-inventory stuff was far more baffling.

Aside from inventory, there is also the exact nature of the stuff in my life. The unanswered *why* questions. It was one of those stories about making whipped cream. There is this point when the cream gets whipped beyond return and starts to turn to butter. My dad would simplify the observation, "This is a bakery, not a creamery. Whipping cream is valuable, butter is useless." Value is driven by the exact nature of what you set out to make.

Taking inventory with an honest perspective of intention and outcomes has produced an asset base that is appropriate filling for cream puffs. Whipping cream works, butter does not! When I learned to identify which actions of mine, intentional or unintentional, caused the cream to turn to butter, then I could no longer blame the ingredients or the bowl temperature or the distraction or the education or the recipe or the time constraints—then the truth was liberating. When you know what you've done, you can make adjustments. There is a keeping track of what works and what doesn't. Each lesson made the recipe better. Taking inventory is both fearless and moral. It counts and drops the plumb line for the foundation of recovery.

5 *Stepping Stone*

After many years of dining for advantage, I believed that good cooks had secret recipes. Growing up in a bakery nurtured the belief that cooks told you enough to keep you stupid and, thus, unable to get a recipe right. Success was a secret, and failure was public.

It took thirty years to understand why my father was generous with his recipes. The lesson was that secret recipes tend to be about shortcuts, substitutions, artificial flavourings—a general cheapening of the product. I learned to share as a child, but as an adult, I learned that really sharing takes telling the whole story, giving them the whole recipe. Before entering treatment, when I told half-truths and used shortcuts, there were a lot of spoiled batches, missed meals, bad days! Early in my recovery journey, I believed my version of the truth, my secret recipe. I believed my lies! On many occasions, I gave long explanations about what I was not going to do.

The secret of being a good baker is in the intuition, in the listening, in taking the directions and following them carefully. The bending toward every waft of air that delivers the smell of fresh pie.

In recovery, I had to revisit the learnings of my youth and sort through the multiple personalities of my emerged self. I learned that each story I told in recovery had the same personality. The recipe was a simple truth. I was glad some moments, mad in others, sad about certain events, and afraid of certain consequences. Giving up the secret recipe and all the formulas for control was liberating.

I spent years fearing the face-wash of the pies of failure. Surrender created not only freedom from self but an awareness that the whole story mattered if I was going to eat great pie. The blend of tart and sweet flavours creates the feast. The juxtaposition of joy and sorrow is the journey. Some years ago, a dear friend of mine died in recovery from an aggressive form of leukemia. We had travelled together in Asia and America. Losing him was sad. My friend hated monkeys, was creeped by them. My friend was also mischievous, repeatedly altering documents and headgear to suit the season appropriately and inappropriately. Picture us in India wearing tea cozies.

And here is where the glitch kicks in—the juggling of joy and sorrow! I took the opportunity with his friends and former partner to sprinkle some of his ashes in a monkey forest in Kathmandu. It was payback time. Joy was complete because the sorrow was real. This was no secret recipe. The laughter was mischievous, and we had the last laugh, for now! The exact recipe for grieving is no secret!

6 *Deleting Defects*

I spent a few years in the music industry back when records were the medium. Yes, that was before CDs and before iSteal and before digital files. I was on a buying trip to New York. It was a Friday afternoon, and we had spent the day sorting through pallets of records with the goal of assembling a semitrailer load of "wax," as we affectionately called records.

Now defective records were hard to sell. They had no market. However, in between the stacks were thousands of deleted albums. Product record companies had culled from their catalogues because sales were minimal. Each deleted album was marked with a double burn scar on the album spine or a hole drilled in the upper right-hand corner through boxes of twenty-five records at a time. This was a bit like going to the Value Village of vinyl. By the very nature of the warehouse, this was about defects and deletes.

If I were to examine my character, I would find many scratched traits not dissimilar to the records in Manny's warehouse. After a few hours of sorting and creating pallets of product, it was time to sit down with Manny.

We had amassed, by greed and good fortune, an entire forty-foot trailer of vinyl records. In an attempt to close the deal and see if there was room for price improvement, I asked Manny if he could agree to unit-price the shipment at twenty cents an album.

Without a word, Manny took a drag on his oversized cigar, swung around in his swivel chair, and with his back to us, said, "It's Friday, and Sabbath begins in an hour. These are deleted records, defective, and you want to bargain for a better price? Defects are only valuable if you get rid of them. Take the whole trailer load at ten thousand dollars, and I can go home happy." A quick calculation confirmed that Manny had not lowered his price. In fact, it was three dollars higher for the entire trailer.

We looked at the clock, and then we looked at Manny's back with a smoke halo circling his curly locks, and all I could say was "Done!" Manny simply swivelled around in his chair, and I wrote the cheque. As I was writing, he said, "I will throw in the freight because to get rid of this load of defects before Sabbath is worth losing a few bucks." Defects of character hang around like bad vinyl, and if you don't move it quickly, it warps useless. Letting go of defects requires knowing what you have and being willing to pay the freight to move it out!

13

7 *Stepping Wolf*

In recovery, I learned that my shortcomings had God appeal. In the many politically corrected versions of children's stories published in the past twenty years, the wolf still eats the princess or blows the house down or chases the little girl with the fascinator—something comes to an end. There is no politically correct way to die. However, I learned that there is a more wholesome way to live. Writing the wolf out of the story means I don't need to be strong. Is it possible, even conceivable, that the wolf needs to eat? The wolf needs to encounter resistance. It took years in recovery to understand that the wolf is stalking and waiting to blow my house down. Waiting for a moment of weakness. Believing that requires a leap more bold than any fable.

I remember the empty flour sacks in the back corner of the bakery. My mother managed the store inventory with the precision of a computer, forty years before they were geek garage projects. Any leftovers were sold as day-old the next day and given away the day after to anyone in need. There was not a lot of waste.

However, my father, for the sake of risk and adventure, would from time to time produce more products than my mother ordered. The argument would roll with her telling him that he never listened and him telling her not to be so cautious because you can't grow a business that way. This is where the flour sacks come in.

When my father was right, he would celebrate and take us out for ice cream. When he was wrong, he would quietly dry the buns and cakes and put the overage into the flour sacks in the back corner of the bakery. My uncle would come into town once a month and look in the back corner of the bakery. When there were a lot of flour sacks in the corner, he'd say, "Not enough listening, too much gambling." While loading the bags into his truck, he would say, "With your shortcomings gone, my pigs will go hungry."

It is a two-edged sword. The wolf needs to eat. We like hero stories—but for the sake of balance, coming up short on crying wolf might help nurture compassion rather than fiction.

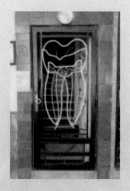  

8 Stepping Gates

In the midseventies and early eighties, there were a significant number of media exposés of governments acting without regard to law. They were breaches of the trust the people had given them. Some of these were known as Watergates, media-gates, and even into the more recent past, as WikiLeaks—each more damaging and cynic making than the previous version, and now in a "postgates" era, we are confronted with the difficulty of discerning who was harming whom.

In the old days (pre-PC), there was this simple rule of 250 that salespersons used to establish networks or spheres of influence. The macchiato crowd has subverted that practicality with a more subtle social functioning and Facebook "friending." The old rule simply said the average wedding and the average funeral were attended by 250 people. I am not sure what the average number of Facebook friends people have; however, I suspect, with the anonymity factor, it has grown well beyond 250. The point of all this has to do with setting some goals for spheres of influence—how many people are cursed by our way of death or how many people are blessed by our living.

I was in the Everglades in Noosa last year, and the reflections of the above-ground vegetation as below-water images stirred a spiritual awareness that silenced my mind. *Contentment* is a good word. The calmer the water, the deeper the reflection. When I put the canoe paddle into the water, the ripple of currents and eddies created by the motion distorted the reflection. In the middle of contemplation, I had to hold on to both ideas to understand the many ways my actions hurt other people. There are circles of influence, and there are ripples in the water.

There is the simple posting of harm, whether on Facebook or by town crier, whether inside families, companies, social networks, or even in imaginary or future relationships. A cause-and-effect relationship.

The deeper awareness came from the paddle in the Everglades. The disturbance of a peaceful balance, the distortion of image-bearing reflection, and the loss of truth are often the greater harm. When the waters are calm, the reflections are a glorious echo of life, and stopping the eddies of gossip requires that I live righteously.

9 *Brewing Coffee*

The old pilgrim Psalter, the Hebrew Psalter, and, for that matter, most religious literature recorded prior to the Common Era, contains the language of Psalm 90, which states, "Hours and days and years are fading." There is finiteness to life on earth. I am going to die. So the psalmist, in "trembling agony," seeks a way to be reconciled to God. My life was lived a quart short on goodness and a little dark on reflecting glory. And then the light goes on. There is, as some recovery literature puts it, a "pained look" in people around us. My behaviour hurt them. There is some sense in which we are inclined by sloth and fear to ignore the warring signs and carry on as if nothing happened. This pained awareness of the shrinking gap between gratitude and contempt is most vivid when I review the new situations in my life.

A few years ago, I had the chance to visit Sierra Leone and my children and grandchildren. With great white expectations, I assumed there would at least be water or at least a restaurant or at least a road or at least something familiar. The absence of the expected and the unspoken contempt are a bit like being an immigrant.

Upon arriving in Canada, my dad bought fresh bananas in the train station in Montreal. This was the land of milk and honey. When he went to work a week later in Burnaby digging peat, this was a cursed place.

When I first landed in the rooms of recovery, I thought this was a foreign land. Concepts of *time* and *mine* were no longer according to my expectations. The very idea of actually telling someone that the wrong was my doing was physically sick-making. I had never done anything wrong in my life.

I knew from all the early-mornings standing across the bakery table from my dad that mistakes were lessons. I lived as if that were a lie. I knew from a flattened pew butt that God was loving and kind, but I lived as if it were a lie. The immigrant kid that landed in recovery needed to take those early lessons and practice newcomer acceptance.

One morning in the bakery, a fellow church elder came to visit my dad. It was four thirty Saturday morning, and 240 loaves of dough were rising on the benches. The pans were greased. The steam was rising from the proofer. Mark walks in and opens the conversation, "Baker, have you got a few minutes? I need some help with . . ." That "few minutes" conversation lasted forty minutes. I scaled the bread alone; I kneaded the pieces of dough into loaves, I panned the loaves' seams down, and, just as Mark was leaving, put the straps of bread into the proofer. As he was leaving, Mark said, "Thanks for showing me how simple it can be to be nice. I'll go home and make her coffee." Dad never said a word. He walked over to the kettle and made us a morning coffee, a coffee we shared whenever the bread was in the proofer. He looked in the proofer, drank coffee, and we talked about stuff. An hour later, he pulled 240 loaves of bread from the oven and smiled. Sometimes, entering foreign territory doing new things, amending our view of the world, is as simple as making bread, as simple as making coffee, as simple as changing the old patterns. The words of the psalmist about *hours and days* keep ringing in my ears whenever I don't take action on an opportunity to change and when I let the land mines of fear explode in my head.

19

10 *Stepping Tenses*

Being raised in a "reformed" family has a way of staining your worldview so that no matter what happens, the dye of experience fades into the fabric of living as threads of origin holding things together. Wandering across the red sands of Sri Lanka, an old strand becomes very clear. My mother would often blend two threads of truth with the translated idioms, "God helps those who help themselves" and "Pray and work." These red sands, these people, this country needed more than a prayer.

At each daily intersection of the threads of my life, I know that my believing and living are woven into patterns of doing and that the spaces, the unknowns, the emptiness are where worry creeps in—where I stop believing that the canvas is a masterpiece, where I want the artist to paint a picture that matches the furniture of my living.

I remember, two years ago, being invited to eat a noon meal with the residents of a monastery. I sat down to eat with my plate on my lap, not speaking a word of Sinhalese We were welcomed, enfolded, and guided through rituals and practices by individuals who showed us what to do, the rituals and language unfamiliar. We were welcomed, and the meal became a journey of discovery. There, the elder monk held the lid of the stew pot open. Beside me, a young girl giggled.

Sitting in temples and churches of every stripe, brand, and flavour has driven a pattern into the tapestry of my faith—the unpredictable threads of language and ritual and welcoming. I became grateful that I was invited into their experience. I was woven into the thread of their fabric. My whiteness and doubtful glances at the food and the hand-washing rituals created the experience for them and for me. We shared their meal. I was invited into the circle, and they treated me as their guest with dignity and without condescension. No apology for their practice, no change.

In my years in NA, no one ever changed the language or diluted the principles. Someone always opened the book to help a newcomer learn the unique language of recovery. In the learning, there was a bonding that lessened my importance and highlighted the life-and-death value of the group norms, language, and practice.

Somehow, the language of our own self-awareness needs to be clear and incisive. We need to look at our living without "dumbing" it down. Recovery is first and foremost a dialogue between a higher power and the beloved. We invite everyone to witness that dialogue and become inspired to enter into fellowship with us. And entering into fellowship, joining in a dialogue with God, has history, roots, and spirited contemporary relevance. Taking stock of my current reality has repeatedly saved my knees from permanent damage, going to bed with the veil of the day torn away by an awareness of how my threads made the pattern of living a little brighter.

11 *Walking in Step*

Sometimes waiting for a plane or camel or glacier can seem like a forever-ticking chunk of time, a block lost to the greying hairline and skyline. I was reminded of this incessant requirement for patience for waiting, sitting at the airport in Agadir. Now this was not your bustling metropolitan melding point. The security inspection was casual. We went in and out of the security zone with chips and with water, each trip precipitated by the ennui of the long-hall waiting. There were no children screaming. In a corner, a man simply spread his djellabas on the ground to pray.

There wasn't a plane in sight. Not even a landing light over the runway. Daylight had gone to fade, and there across the terrazzo floor, a soccer ball rolled. It wasn't really round. It was the saltwater-shrunken round of twenty teams playing at the tide line at dawn.

There they played a game with field boundary lines scratched into a perfect pitch by sticks and the goalposts spaced to challenge team skills. They knew you could adjust the goalposts without changing the game.

Now this memory was brought to mind by a ticking clock (what delusional notion of time and technology makes it necessary to have a ticktock sound come from an electronic clock?) while I was sitting at an empty table before dawn in the Terrace airport. Fresh snow everywhere. No plane in sight. No runway. Miles from the beaches of Morocco. The only thing visible across the horizon was a haloed moon.

Daylight was coming soon, even on these—the shortest northern days of the year. In the closet, a golden soccer ball and, resting on the carpet, a mini soccer ball almost permissible for inside use. This waiting business has more to do with escape than time. It has to do with accepting the changes in the game, in the game plan! The fresh snow has an immediate way of bringing the present forward. A snap to reality. Snow wraps the sound of wheels and pads the voices. Between the clock ticks and the softened silence of an awakening city, there is no waiting. Sometimes there is the quiet hope that the plane won't come, and some winter storm will bind us over for a week of cabin fever and snow shovelling. Then the cursed reality of waiting for the next flight out of here sets in, and then a grateful thank-you for the moments of grace overwhelms.

We drive back to the house and gather around the couch. *Sitting* is not a word I would use as the mélange of intertwined bodies bends toward the available light to read in the silence, savouring a galaxy of imaginary worlds without sharing words.

The snow accumulates, and we begin clearing a patch of driveway—not for the car but for the soccer ball—and on the snow banks, the cheerleading angels are waved into existence by arms. This is Advent. I was waiting for a way out and learned again that my ideas of waiting or of angels or Jesus were empty. When I adjusted the goalposts and brought my soccer ball to the game, I made a spiritual connection. I learned, ticking slowly, that God shows up in a snowfall or a garden or a mall or a shelter. This getting-good-with-God stuff is not about waiting, but more about seeing that God is OK with me! All I need to do is wait expectantly.

12 *Stepping Out*

The give and take that we accept about life is practically very complicated. No amount of preached simplicity holds water. With predictable regularity, the sun comes up, and light emerges from the darkness; yet every morning, I open the curtains to check that it is so. A momentary pinch of the mental cheeks to confirm that we have survived another night, that I am still alive and actually need to do something. This latter is the curse of living and its richest blessing.

I was a kid in high school, and on Wednesday and Friday mornings, I would ride my bicycle to the bakery at 4:00 a.m. to give my dad a break so he could sleep till seven. Now as a high school kid, riding a bicycle for ten minutes was no major chore. Riding it in the rain at 4:00 a.m. created these wonderful cursing bits of dialogue about how unfair it was, and why I needed to do this, and why my dad didn't have a regular job, and even the muttering about why he spent so much time on Tuesday and Thursday nights at church meetings. Why did he make time for everybody else?

Once I got the bread dough mixed and the batches of sweet dough started, the routines carried me through till my dad arrived at seven. He quietly put on the coffeepot, walked over to each proofing mound of dough and gently pinched it for texture, temperature, and time. There was this moment of pride when, already knowing I had done a good job, he would say, "I guess we've earned a cup of coffee by now." We would pause for a coffee and the rambling morning conversation that poured a whole night of restlessness between us. We shared stories.

Many times, the characters were nameless when he told stories of visiting sick or dying or otherwise hurting persons. Other times, they were glorious celebrations about a new immigrant family having found a place to live or a job or a school.

The recovery notions of carrying a message, of sharing a bit of hope, of lightening the load of someone's journey with a smile, with a coffee and a conversation has its roots in human kindness. The kindergarten notions of sharing your toys, sharing your snacks, giving your friend the crayon because her picture is more important than yours—each is a prayer without words.

The other night, I was having a conversation with someone who had just visited with a group of inmates in a federal institution, and he said that the highlight of his week was when the new guy, who had just read some recovery literature for the first time, declared that this not only described who he was, but also explained his life. The inmate is still an inmate. The sun did come up again, but my friend understood why he got up that day. Doing something that carries the very reasons for living to the practical hearts of the world—that is a spiritual practice that not any prayer mat, seminar, church, temple, or cathedral can deliver.

On one of those early childhood mornings, I remember feeling extremely happy and singing something as I was riding along. The sun was not up yet, but I knew that by the time my dad walked through the door and poured coffee, this was going to be a great day. Changing the course of someone's day has a way of building anticipation that it might happen again. That's faith. Changing the course of your day to stop for coffee just to listen, that builds hope.

13 Sidestepping

I need to tell you about the morning some months ago when I heard the pea gravel crackle underfoot, ripping through the 6:00 a.m. silence like cheap chalk. The sun was cresting the horizon and warming everything as a delicate wisp of mist ascended and vanished in the sounds of kettles and gravel. There is nothing special about this morning, except that I was emerging from a boxcar. Spending a night in a railcar on a siding without tracks has a way of focusing place, a way of grounding.

You need to capture this moment with me. When I was a kid, my dad would regularly stop baking on any given day and wash the car. Where we grew up, a West Coast rain could show up anytime and render washing a car useless. The reward of some sudden downpour and the subsequent road dirt splattered across the doors and fenders muted the vanity before anyone could see the clean car.

The sun comes up and the rain comes down. Every child knows this, sings this, lives to dance between puddles and beaches. The effort my dad put into washing the car was the same effort he put into planting flowers and decorating a cake. Yet he knew that the car would get dirty, the flowers would wither and die, and the cake would get eaten.

As a child growing up, I believed that the pea gravel of a Thetis Island beach was the announcement of summer. Hearing the rocks crushing underfoot when I emerged from the railcar was a reminder that all those lessons, all that learning, all that experience belonged together.

It took me years to learn that my father savoured life in the moment—from the kitchen to the garden, from the glory of nature to the grand scales of music. He would rather play the organ than dry dishes. He would rather water the garden than sit still. He would rather carve a flower-bed border with a spade than read a book.

As my father was dying, he lay singing a doxology from memory. The marvellous part was that he learned the song as a kid from his dad, memorized it in church, played it as the dishes dried, and punctuated every task with the practice of contentment. He never distinguished his beliefs from his practice. He walked through death, war, and immigration learning with each step to walk the talk.

The gift of recovery is more than an academic statistic that proves recovery works. Working the first twelve steps and living into the changes deliver change. There are some twenty-seven million persons living in recovery in North America, each evidence that people do recover. The pea gravel crushing underfoot was worn round by centuries of water and waves. Living spiritually balanced lives has everything to do with consistently doing the right thing. Washing the car because it makes some corner of your life more pleasing. Visiting a sick person in a hospital to share conversation. Attending a jail meeting to be the presence of hope. Hiking the mountain trail to see the majestic. Playing with a child and laughing. Singing a deathbed doxology.

This postscript numbered 13 could become a moralizing judgment or a prayer that your life might be lived with a spiritual practice that restores virtue, proves forgiveness, and grants freedom from regret and shame. Living right is the best revenge!

There were many Saturday evenings when I was young that we'd all had our Saturday evening bath after a day in the bakery. Shedding the sugar and yeast odours in a bath was a preparatory ritual for Sunday—but also for Saturday night. We were never granted television viewing time without our parents present, and the black-and-white was only on for maybe two hours a week. Saturday evening after the dishes were done, the baths done, and the schoolwork checked, the five of us would gather around the screen as if Messiah had come and watch the next episode of *Gunsmoke*. The predictable ending of each episode was the expectation. My dad put it simply, "It's good to do the right thing." May the music of the steps accompany you until you die!

STRENGTH

Because if metaphor is one of the ways we have left to approach God, to begin to understand faith, memory itself is a living metaphor of eternal life . . . Loss brings pain. Pain triggers memory... And memory is a kind of new birth . . . And that new birth after long pain . . . That resurrection—in *memory*—that comforts us . . . Teaches us something about eternal life . . . Remember . . . Memory changes pain to laughter and joy . . . To bring the dead (stuff) back to life in our lives.

—*Sue Miller in While I Was Gone*

1

Shalom

This man has done nothing . . . I tell you . . . today you will be wwith me in paradise.

—*Luke 23:41–43*

a few foot blocks of Main Street will open
your eyes to the bent-end of time n space

the picture of crumbled creatures telling
news about running out of mace n face
is a moving painting—chalked on the city street
an image of tired people running toward empty

yet there that grin and the other smiling
together about the few drops of liquid grace
leftover behind the Only Restaurant broken
like bread and wine poured-hope shared delivery
from the fade-by-years pained memory of missing
sons n daughters each reaching for home base

right now without an outstretched arm
they eat n drink in their own paradise

Waiting

what if the building blocks of my believing
were shaken by an earthquake a trembling killer
from the very bowels of my firm foundation
would I be still have faith and sing

the blood of your torn flesh—stains
the trembling words you use between the pauses
as you curse creation for every broken rib
—the dry bones that made "him" king

then stooped down to the red earth bending
your formed words into a prayer—heart screaming
to reach across an ocean of tears
empty like a bathtub—you're left with a ring

in this promised world there is no sea
and the ring of your prayer will be empty

2 *Monkey Moniker*

The peace of God that passes our understanding.

—*Philippians 4:7*

the seated five-year-old kid drooling dried blood
tonsils clipped
            scaled dream disproportionate
in the oversized smoker chair
across the armrest on a supported board
the wind-up monkey turns somersaults
as images of ether gas and stainless spittoons
whirl through the pain-fogged child
recovering memories

fifty-two years later, the boy recovers memory,
a mechanical monkey in a window
on Sutter Street

the clang and click of the clipping
a reverberating cable car of memory
hauled up and down the hills of a haunted past
a brief presence

tears wash awareness into the moment
and the boy emerges an empty older
wishing and wanting whatever was
waiting again for some toy to take away the pain,
distracted—long enough for the racing rails of thought
to silence in the approaching evening air

no toys, no games, no sights, no thrills
have ever clutched across the empty gulch
only the thousand moments of her presence
have delivered delighted prayer and peace

his soul is at rest in her presence,
a window of hope—a radiant glow
watching him wander waitingly
through the lonely hours,
bridging the ravines of living
with the verdant valleys
of their coming together

knowing possibility and impossibility
nurturing hope and trust
speaking with flesh what words won't

unwinding the springs of time
then reaching through history
into the outstretched arms of presence
a peace that passes understanding

3 Thanka Painting

When people follow the law . . . by instinct . . . they confirm its truth by their living.

—*Romans 2:14*

Bare-bulbed filament
lights the path the finger traces,
unlike the details in the *thanka* painting,
the light and her words are sparse.

Her finger carves the curves of a cosmology
stroked by nearly bald brushes—
a fascinating crossover without a cross,
a death-defying miracle with five heads,
a world woven together with serpent tales,
and picturing spirals of forever.

There was resurrection in her eyes,
she got up once more
to do the simple brushstrokes,

to tell the story of her imagined life,
to spread the challenge of her desire,
godlike, laying everything out
with paints on a palette,
with finger-pointing
and then waiting for the first strokes
the bells of midnight
      the inspiration to fire the filament
      the dream to shake the firmament.

4 *Our Father*

who art in heaven,
rising months have passed
since we last shared words—baked bread
and the prayer lingers
like an almighty hug.

Quietly sliding your feet
in a baker's practised shuffle
across the threshold of life
and then entering the piped passage—
      a spreading palette smoothing every imperfection

The layers of cake,
each a berry-coated practice canvas,
a practical lesson,
each covered with a halo
of sweet perfection.

Sketches of yard designs and cakes
marked with penciled, clear, pathways
between the beds of flowers and fields of grass
walkways widening, curved with a spatula
leading to the door.

That was your way,
scribbling with ever-dull pencils,
      the lead icing squeezed by your kneading hand
as a sculpted vision,

rearranging pathways, plants, and pastries,
making something new.

In margins, the notes and memories are buried—
scratches in the recipes and music
each alteration—a freshness,

a whole new song,
a prayer for shalom.

Hallowed be your name
with each stopped tear
that is lowered to the ground
into your kingdom come
carried in a coffin—
holding memories.

No notes—not even a few chords
only a fresh inventory
only today's daily bread!

5 *Forever*

Because if metaphor is one of the ways we have left to approach God, to begin to understand faith, memory itself is a living metaphor of eternal life . . . Loss brings pain. Pain triggers memory . . . And memory is a kind of new birth . . . And that new birth after long pain . . . That resurrection—in *memory*—that comforts us . . . Teaches us something about eternal life . . . Remember . . . Memory changes pain to laughter and joy . . . To bring the dead (stuff) back to life in our lives.

—*Sue Miller in While I Was Gone*

reading the words
opened a whole catalogue of dead-end
moments of loss
weeks of regret
      the memories of should've, would've, could've
      and the piled-up guilt packed into the
suitcases of attics past
      the escaped wonders
      the unchased dreams
      the rainbow showers
      the drawling shadows
      the wandering mysteries
      the standing strong
      the fallen weak
      the stunning beauties
      the sparkling minds
      the open coffins
and   the closed chapters

savouring the images in moments of recall
memory pauses at your side
and sees more than a still image
rather a moving stream of pixels
cascades across the synapses

and there, where time pauses
was a whole savoury world
served to the senses

what was secret has become openness
that is shared like intimate nakedness—
a gift between associates
who, like students, have graduated
cap in hand
gown lifted to navigate the steps of life
ready chapters in books of memory
living into the fullness of time
writing new pages when we meet

6 *Tracking a Hungry World*

flipping through the mind's album
the railcar years pass
through junctions and sidings of rest
carrying live cargo

picking up speed as the grade
passes from plateau to valley
slowing to climb mountain mirages
limited by understanding

whistling for that next crossing
where words will stop
and wait for time to pass
lights flashing a level warning

lowering the barricades
on the last barb
as the engine rolls
every phrase flat like a sermon

on the tracks where we walk
the shining rail arcs to the left
polished by wheels
scoring each note in steel

the photo doesn't print clear
into memory—rather it fuses
colours and figures
years softened the outlines of bodies

the young heifer and steer
bounced dead by a slow freight
is that you and I shaking
are we huddled in the bed

bodies grinding in the rocks
knowing we missed the freight
counting the petals of days
rattled flower children

each coloured flag
surrendered to the ground
loves me—loves me not
and then starting for home again

fear held us together tighter
than a woman grips her first lover
losing everything for nothing
tension torn together

an impressionistic collage
scraps recycled
without a deposit program
wet grain cars swelling on the siding

waiting for the power to move
as we would wait—nights for a child
to be born, to come home, to leave
life bruised by water and time

in the corner a scrap driven
by spikes into beams—your head
leaning toward the camera
a red-eyed flash

a smile breaks that crescent
and your new dress
the first dress you made
needles endlessly breaking

well into the night cursing singer
torn into the middle a fragment
a baptismal gown
flowing—foreshadowing

the tracks are quiet now
some Swiss welding has clicked
every clack out of existence
there are still pauses in the words between us

growing longer like a freight train
without a caboose in sight
uncertain of the end yet knowing it comes
like the cars the kids counted

7 *High Top Healing*

the steps lead like all steps—down
beneath the obvious
a peeling away of pretension
a removal—a voiding of
all that does not belong
a clean emptiness
leading a going down
and there scratched like memory
on the cellar steps
on the road to Kathmandu
hanging against the grey cement
shadowed with bareness
footprint holders
high tops for great heights
the highest high tops
drying like step works
in the step well of tears
ready to climb onto feet again
to run in your race

8 *Our Mother on Earth*

we lost another mother
not surprising
she'd been fading away for days
cheating the promised stretch
of just some months more

she died quietly, after having lived
stronger than memory
mothering her sons
and smothering grandchildren with love
knowing all will be well!

this is not just another death
this is mother—gone forever
her testament engraved
with the keen edge of her tongue—
you'll be all right without me now

she'd talk about her sons—
their driven impatience—her own
their gentleness—her own
their persistence—her own
their accomplishments and failures—her own

she carried them close, as only a mother can
hugging them
taking the good and the bad and always loving
she spoke softly when concerned
the boys needed her—each in their own way

she died last night—nine forty-five
it was like the clock stopped
and she didn't—her memory
her footprints clearly moving
always knowing

no matter how great the hurdle
she lived completely
in this world—the tears of suffering
are notes on another scale
waiting for accompaniment

she sang in her failing breath
the first song without tears

9

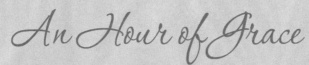

An Hour of Grace

Connecting to your eyes over blackberries
gazing at the ripeness—the beginning
with longing, I know for sure
a person does not have time for everything.

How can one love and regret at the same time?
How can one laugh and cry with the same eyes,
with the same hand-snap fabric and hold on,
make love in war and fight in love?

This tension between erased forgiveness and snapshot remembrance
to eat and digest what history will not forget
to make amends without lamenting loss
and finding that forgetting begins without end.

The tension between the longing and the belonging
stretches the possibilities—we were good to each other
enfolded in discovery and enriched by pleasure
only our souls experienced everything!

The body tries to hold on, draw closer, tug
muddled between pinnacles of pleasure and gouges of pain
and we accept each other healing
in an hour of grace—a giftedness

where there is time for everything—
a moment borrowed from eternity
to dream the awakening impossibility
and play in fields of grace.

10 *Insight*

Blessed are you if you sow seed by streams
and let your oxen range free.

—*Isaiah 32:20*

the price of a team of oxen   like cab fare
is fixed at the city gate   each trader
seeking a matched pair in genetic combinations
infinite with impossibility

there's one—a straight back
solid hindquarters   a family history
of devoted service   the mandatory
disclosure didn't include the goring

stirring the dust with your sandal
thrown on the ground you seal
the exchange with all the ring
of a marriage ceremony

in the square it's easy to buy oxen
with childlike innocence believing
a perfect team exists   yet   the farmer
spends history looking for power

to plough a field without wandering
left or right   years of ploughing words
striking stones and drawing into ruts
turning sheets like sod and harrowing

nights have strained my nuptial eyes
the yoke of childhood lessons
that reigns (always rearranging)
my shoulders calloused

by a burden borne between us
a harness that holds back
restrains   slows   I believed
in redemption   having learned early

that it was a handout like the scissor-cut coupons
or the quarter thrown in the hat
each epistle clipped into memory
by pounding fists punctuating

words that promised change
I learned freedom—waiting for change
that was never thrown my way
instead—discovering her unharnessed in a field

a scene drawn from a dream by drying eyes
dripping words that mattered
when you throw your flight coupons
on the counter—exchanging

won't lift the yoke you crawl under
shifting will not lighten the weight
you feel   dancing can't match
the spring calf you envy

redemption is not a handout
luring with promises of a perfect team
rather   it's a turning freely
in fields without the chaffing—

chasing dreams without sleeping
and sowing seeds by streams
never returning for harvest

11 *The Phone Rings*

Yet I am not silenced by the darkness . . . the thick darkness
that covers my face.

—*Job 23:17*

the ducking ugliness
that only a cell phone can cut into peace
disturbed everything and more

the doctor
wanting your number—
without words explained in the questions
        you were missing—
        lost in an escape from your Alcatraz
        dreaming that the you could cross the ocean
        to safety—
        use once more successfully
where the living
        you coaxed with hope
        have learned
and the dog-tagged dead
        who drowned in a vomit of fear
        have succumbed

you were my friend, my redeemer
        who counseled and travelled
        miles of recovery road
        into living and enjoying

the emptiness
        of hundreds of lonely nights
        locked behind doors of self
        barricaded by the mind's police

crushed by remonstrance of self-pity
escaping nothing in a chemical fog of fear
the distance of desperation
and the words of requiem
poured into remembrance
like yesterday
and between the waterless tears
the fear spoke without words—

you could die
bloody well poke yourself to death
do an eternal hopeless whack

i was afraid, am afraid
of demising you like a wall
from my life
and more afraid of the end that always comes
when the road home is too hard

i spoke words into an empty room
cursed and prayed
running the programs of promise
and the lessons of experience

waiting for the phone to ring
its ugly, disturbing worst

just to hear your voice would be hope

the ominous silence of the dial tone
carved a festering hole in the day
i broke words to the remnants of your partner
she sobbed for miles, tearing the worst
knowing nothing more than emptiness and the rags of history

speak words into the night
pray in that dark garden for the cup to pass
come home to rest, my friend
before the end

12 *Flagellation*

after seeing Rembrandt's painting with the same struck-name

the strokes of your brush   delicately
trace the curves in the skeleton
covering flesh where the strikes
of the whip should have scored the skin

each scratch exposes your brushed
observation of the whipped model
such softly rounded cheeks
and a powdered   beardless face

shuttling through the tapestry of theology
and unmasking the humbled Jesus
who didn't whimper before Pontius Pilate
your statement fleshes out the mystery

the preservation light of the gallery
shows with brush-traced strokes
a feminine side of the humbled body
that returned from the whipping

you brushed the imagined question
did Caesar's Roman agents flog a woman
the betrayed face   returning from the worst
beating on earth is the bride without veil

both history and theology are burdened
with inerrant facts but void of mystery

on your canvas   Rembrandt
you stroked
the miracle of conception
whipped by time
into a story

the miracle of Mary Magdalene
dragged from a lover's bed

the miracle of Mary Magdalene
alone   sharing blushed cheeks
with the gardener

13 *Wisdom*

for David and Jan

always wanting, after forty-five years,
still wanting to declare death as unnatural
out of order
dead child was only two

in the slush of snow, we carried the body
in a scaled casket to a dirt grave
six men stumbling
to stop the tears of watching

the end comes quite naturally
slowly, quickly, early, late
like a crop yielding to seasons
gathered without prayers into barns

his boxer's eyes (alive to the end)
guiding the poles that support
the distended stomach, liver, and spleen
all overgrown with cancerous weeds

each cell a sentenced lifer, waiting for mercy
killing off a young body so naturally
if you only knew who to blame
if only there were the right answers

nature and supernature handled
separately by theological systems
but each rising and falling, like breath

in lungs, ends in the same box
counting days is no longer
something one learns like math in school
rather, each year we announce approaching death
with a numbered hallmark of gaiety
that is normally reserved for drafty bars,
for floats in parades
and smouldering barbecues

yet the finger writes on the granite tablets

a broken numbering
an end beckoning with new orders
the mother with empty arms (too short to reach his body)
always keeps stretching for another day,
one more breath before her own death

death comes as promised
in time her laughter fails
and tears sting her silk blouse—indelible marks
ground into fabric
fabric into ground

PRAYERS

Opening

God, be merciful
we are rattled by this week in your presence
the table of your presence is set
there is sickness there is death
there is sunshine there is laughter
there are tears there are friends
there are children there is music
there is bread

God, be merciful
we confess our difficulty with acceptance
we wrestle your holy presence in our unholy lives
feed us
with loving humility   with caring compassion
with giving generosity   with quiet kindness
with armed comfort   with focused faithfulness
with strengthening laughter

God, be merciful
we stand in awe of your forgiveness
the arms stretched toward us
encouraging lame to walk
lighting the nights of fear
carrying the homeless home
calling the unloved by name
waving signposts of your kingdom
hearing our prayer
for redemption
for freedom

Seeking

the bells and flags and incense
are all prayer monuments to a system of hope
a pattern of assurance
almost archaic for our sophisticated times
prayers whisper, wave, ring, and mist over us

the primary flags wave in the evening as the leeward wind changes
miles of colour woven in the wind
an umbrella catching sunshine and rain
fading into the tropical vegetation

there a bell rings, a gong sounds
somehow the tones echo
and the cymbals
harmonize with a presence blending into the surroundings

somehow the words bear with us in wisps of incense
permeating each petition
blending into the aroma
and there for a moment pause as breath that is stopped

there is a vision of all right
a glimpse of glory, a shudder of delight
flags waving without mast or master
announcing a fair weathering

winds of change
riding beside us and ringing history
the bells peal back doubt and layer the promises in our ears
resounding fundamental hope

Surrendering

Echoes of an Ancient Prayer

Holy One, in a world screaming for attention
Make me an instrument of your peace.
    I face you—naked and ashamed
    You were with me, and I never knew you—
    that hungry brother, that wounded sister!
Where there is hatred, let me sow love
    Teach me to love my enemies
Where there is doubt about what good God is
    teach me to speak of my experience
    with your faithfulness
Where there is despair—the dying from hunger, thirst, pain, grief
    show me the presence of new beginnings
    teach me to speak of the hope
    of my resurrection from the dead
Where there is sadness
    let me deliver the joy of your presence
Where there is darkness
    let me blaze a trail of holy light

Grant that I may not seek to be consoled
> teach me to console
> send me into your world
> to comfort, hold, shelter, soothe, and warm

Grant that I may not seek to be understood
> teach me to understand
> send me into your world
> to listen, consider, accept, honour, acknowledge, and esteem

Grant that I may not seek to be loved
> teach me to love
> send me into your world
> to care, share, bear, admire, and adore

In giving, we receive
> teach me to give up everything
> family, friends, mothers, brothers, money, jobs
> so I can have everything

In pardoning, we are pardoned
> teach me to forgive as you forgave—
> every little thing—even the bickering gossip

In dying, we are born to eternal life
> join my hands with your children around the world
> open my eyes to the daily miracle of new life
> the gifts of recovery from self

Counting

Holy One, we've been waiting for a miracle . . .
    some lightning bolt of your presence
    just to let us know that
    we can count on your mighty ways
    we really are a gathering of doubting Thomases
    we need evidence, signs, seals, symbols
    anything that lets us know that you are real

Holy One, as we enter each season of waiting
    we want to experience your mighty promised good
    we want more than mangers and babies
    we want an almighty presence in our lives.
    we want to pause and
    recall the hugs from your mothering arms this week

Monday, the list of tasks was longer than the hours
Tuesday, you were there when we laughed
Wednesday, your hand on our shoulder lifting the hundred-pound phone
Thursday, a nasty argument and sending flowers wasn't hard
Friday, a week of unfinished leftovers stuffed in drawers

Holy One, we have experienced your mighty presence . . .
forgive us for taking you for granted
    you preserved us on miles of road
    kept us from famine and pestilence
    comforted us when alone
    delivered healing care
    whether we were ready or not

Sharing

God, today was a gift from your hand
every stroke a sign of genius
the food and drink on these tables
a blessing of your common grace

We give you thanks for the gift of each other
working in community to build bridges of hope
sign posts of freedom from slavery

We pray for every addict still suffering
and give you thanks for this meal
and the 109,000 meals served at Last Door

We give thanks for willing tradespeople
corporations, employers, families, and persons
walking alongside those seeking redemption

Today was a gift from your hand.
We give thanks for this food, these people
and your abundant blessing and compassion

We pray all this, giving thanks in all our living
for all our relations for all your gifts

Repairing

God,
who is not way out there
who is not far away

God,
who we can't understand
until we understand ourselves

God,
who is within ourselves
we come before each other

God,
who holds us in your arms
we acknowledge who you are and who we are

God,
who is the very ground of our lives
an inescapable presence

God,
who can't be manipulated by our prayers
nor can we hide from your face in each other

God,
help us be life-givers
to fulfill our deepest task

God,
help us
give ourselves away

Building

God,
we so often seek you in some distant realm
or some song or hymn or other external dream

God,
show us again today
that you can only be found in our humanity

God,
draw life into our worship
carry us this day with awe and wonder

God, teach us to marvel at the big things:
        the mountains
        the stars
        the trees
        the deserts
        the rivers
        the icebergs
        the beams in our eyes

God, open us to the wonder of the tiny:
        the synapse in a brain cell
        the virus in a chicken
        the sperm swimming to the egg
        the algorithms of the computer
        the harmonics in a song
        the speck in our neighbour's eye

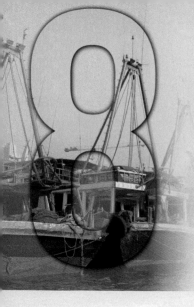

Sentencing

Master, *somewhere in the departing—*
really a dance between wants and desires—
I left a thousand valuables unsaid
summarized in the paragraph of tears
that cross-eyed our path
I want to hear your voice

wandering around, sentenced to my word
i remembered the laughter we shared
the struggling for definition
between my words and yours
the pillow tales
the words in the afterglow of our coming together
sentenced together by the flow of our words
formed for intimacy by the feelings we share
and those we anticipate
the bliss of a special kiss
the stroke of souled affection
all woven into friendship
the sound of water as our feet shared a path
in the descending daylight
there—that bird
beyond the daisies
and then a gentle embrace
the bliss granted us time to feel whole
dancing our own imperfections and knowing
the wonderful—a gift
granted by my higher purpose

we have been sentenced together
by the grace of your words and deeds
grant me your gracious presence
make each departing a fare-thee-well
until we come together again

Changing

great God, teach me *forgiven*
move me beyond my limits
into something more real,
a whole forgiven meal
God be the teacher—show me how to love the sick

God, I have dreams of recovered desires
expose them to truth and bear pain with me
grant doubting faith, ailing health,
renewed hope, and stalled patience
God, I want to stop crying myself to sleep
stop the self-pity
recovering friends and family from abuse and violence

I want to share my darkest fears with you
losing jobs and losing memory
the fear of never being good enough

God, you understand the stains of pain
the fear of being alone, of dying, of losing face

God, help me utter words of truth
about my desires, wants, wishes, hopes, and dreams
teach me to exchange my parcel of guilt
for a voucher of forgiveness

Righting

God, help us heal the brokenness of our kingdoms

teach us to broker peace
between Catholics and Protestants
between Christians and Muslims
between Israelis and Palestinians
between Hindus and Sikhs
between Natives and Immigrants
between Americans and Canadians
between French and English

teach us to free our slaves
whether they be children
smuggled in truckloads to factories for the shoes we wear
or the partner trapped in the kitchen
or the underpaid, riled-at retail clerk
grant them a writ of liberty

teach us again and again by example
the dead end of our ways of thinking and acting
open our eyes to possibilities

God, show us by your calling
our calling, that by our living,
all of creation springs alive in witness to our hope
raise up life as evidence of your restoration
we pray this desiring
to live in peace
to love in righteousness
and to be Christ to the other

Blessing

Creator God, this day again we give you thanks
for granting us another glimpse of your holy will

God, we give you thanks for every inheritance we have
the stories of grace and glory
that binds us as family and friends
that finds us celebrating your presence

God of each and all, take the words woven by our flesh
words wired to this time and place
and make them the quilted threads of our living

Creator God, in the quietest of hours
hear us struggling with acceptance
each longing for our own desires
always having to learn again and again

that acceptance of your holy will
brings an almighty shalom—
a peace that passes understanding

God, free each of us here from the burden of what has been
and lead us lightly—like a cloud
as we search for fire in our souls
unleashing our story into the present

God, hold before us the butterflies of your effect
your changing everything
colouring a world with the passion of compassion

God, grant us your presence to cheer, guide, comfort, and bless
and as we pause to break bread
as we pause to celebrate
we ask your blessing on this meal again

as we learned to pray
Here zegene deze speisen
God bless this food!

Amen

Helping

forty years is a long time for a memory
yet like a birthmark
your unfolding—
the exploration
of that first night
that every boy dreams of
and then never forgets
that moment of desire
was the opening
of a stream of compressed
images

pictures that expand
as time and experience decode
the richness and texture
learning early
to taste and touch
the bud of life

unfolding each time
as fruit follows blossoms
and then savouring the sweetness
always attracted
to the flower
and storing honey

for the winter of memory

when in the approaching darkness
not even memory remains

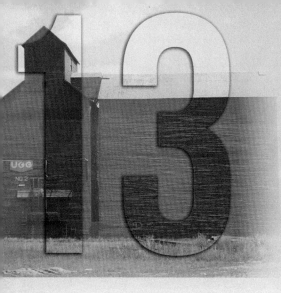

Praying

somehow as the feet pressed cobblestone
they found the Gothic reformation arches

portals that support an entire heaven

Holy One, the forever space between
the grounding marble and the ceiling
grows with noted reverberation

Master, the pipes speak with voiced precision
hymns vaulted to the heavens
tuned to the mystery of living on earth

the organ whispers a symphony of sound
into the space
silencing distance and doubt

God in the curve-carved pew
I kneel alone—praying
across the Babel of distance

the new candle flickers with hope
as the Madonna smiles amen

Epilogue

I think of that Good Friday morning many years ago when my children dragged the remnants of my disease-ravished life from a shooting gallery. There is no doubt that God walks a little closer to the ground than I ever imagined—closer than I ever allowed myself to believe.

Henri Nouwen observes that the victims of poverty and disease are more openly convinced of God's love. In the past eighteen years, I have experienced hundreds of spiritual awakenings in the lives of people who were dying from the consequences of their addictive behaviours. The common theme sounds like this, "I owe my life to the fellowship of . . . because it was here that I learned to live again, to experience life, to feel loved, to eat and drink, to give up my resentments and to experience a new relationship with my higher power."

It's not often we hear that kind of talk in churches, because most of us have some distance, or we think we do, from the peril of our sin. For the recovering addict, or alcoholic or smoker, sex addict or Internet monkey, there is the constant threat of relapse. The threat of reverting to the old ways of life, to stuff the emotional void, is real. The threat of daily struggles with sin is equally real. Those of us who live in the superfluous stuff of first-world living may make our annual gifts to the poor or our crisis visits to the housebound, but the faces often remain as the faces of unknown neighbours. We have never held on to dear life in true companionship.

Henri Nouwen penetrates the veneer with this question, "Why is it that we keep giving dimes to beggars without daring to look into the face of the beggar." When I was dying, God sent my family and friends to sit with me. I didn't listen to their words, but the way their eyes shared my pain, the way their tears rolled, the way they kept listening to the most disjointed logic of my insanity gave me hope. They and many other saints became my companions and sat with me through the darker nights. They entered and joined me in a journey toward wholeness. They came to the hovels of desperation and sat at my bedside. They didn't understand addiction. They just loved me—till I could love myself. This faith business works no matter how dark the night—even if your only song is a scream of pain. An invitation to be in paradise. Those Good Friday glimpses of hope turn into minutes, hours, days, and years in community.

Printed in the United States
By Bookmasters